GUIDE TO DOGS

Wendy Boorer

Illustrated by Roy Coombs

Designed by Jane Olliver

Ray Rourke Publishing Company, Inc.
Windermere, Florida 32786

Published by Ray Rourke Publishing Company, Inc.,
Windermere, Florida 32786.
Copyright © 1979 Grisewood & Dempsey Ltd.
Copyright © 1981 Ray Rourke Publishing Company, Inc.

Library of Congress Cataloging in Publication Data

Boorer, Wendy.
   Guide to dogs.

   (Explorer guides)
   Includes index.
   SUMMARY: Briefly covers the history of dogs, various
breeds, dogs as pets, and the training and care of dogs.
   1. Dogs—Juvenile literature. [1. Dogs] I. Coombs,
Roy.   II. Title.   III. Series.
SF426.5.B66   1981   636.7   81-661
ISBN 0-86592-015-X   AACR2

Contents

About This Book

This book is an introduction to the world of pedigree dogs. It attempts to show the wide variety of breeds available, from the tiny Chihuahua to the huge Irish Wolfhound. As well as discussing the history of the dog and why different types developed, over eighty modern breeds are described and illustrated.

Many aspects of the care of dogs as well as their training are also included. This is an ideal book for the child who wants to know more about how to choose a suitable breed of dog as a pet and how to care for it when they have got it.

All About Dogs

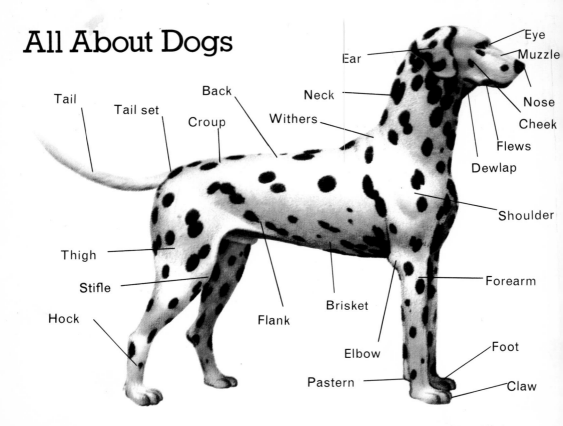

Tail · Tail set · Back · Croup · Withers · Neck · Ear · Eye · Muzzle · Nose · Cheek · Flews · Dewlap · Shoulder · Thigh · Stifle · Hock · Flank · Brisket · Forearm · Elbow · Foot · Pastern · Claw

▲ **A Dalmatian** showing the main features of a dog.

Dogs are intelligent and rewarding companions which have long been useful to man. They were the first animal to be tamed by man. Through the centuries many different breeds have been developed to do different types of work. This is why today there are several kinds of hunting dogs, gundogs, guard dogs, sheep-dogs and others. Different countries have their own range of breeds to do these jobs. For example, looking after sheep in the Welsh mountains is not the same as looking after sheep in the Australian outback. Different types of dog have been bred to suit these types of work.

Very few breeds are used now for the work they were originally bred to do. They are almost all kept as pets or show dogs. Each breed has its own character and appearance and this gives a great variety of choice.

The breeds in this book are divided into six groups according to the kind of work they used to do. These groups are sporting dogs, hounds, terriers, working dogs, toy dogs and utility dogs (which are in the section "Dogs for Pets").

The Speed of Dogs

Borzoi   Saluki   Whippet   Greyhound

The fastest breed of dog is the grey-hound. It can reach speeds of about 35 miles an hour.

Notice that these fast-running dogs have long legs and slender bodies so that they can cover a lot of ground.

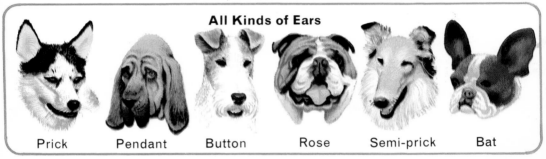

All Kinds of Ears

Prick   Pendant   Button   Rose   Semi-prick   Bat

How Big Are Dogs?

The Chihuahua is the smallest dog in the world. It can weigh as little as 1 lb. St Bernards (see page 14) are the heaviest dogs, weighing as much as 190 lb. The tallest breed is the Irish Wolfhound which stands at least 31 in at the withers. (Dogs are measured from the ground to the withers.) The Shetland Sheepdog is about 14 in high and is a good size for a pet.

Chihuahua

Shetland Sheepdog   Irish Wolfhound

The Dog Family

The dog family includes not only all breeds of dog but all the wild dogs as well. Wolves, foxes, jackals, hyenas and the rest are all related to the dogs we keep as pets: they all belong to the family Canidae.

It is thought that wolves are the closest relatives to domestic dogs. They are social animals, hunting in packs. The domestic dog is a social animal too. This shows in the way he prefers to be with you rather than shut away.

Dogs today are descended from Cynodictus, a prehistoric animal that lived more than two million years ago.

Famous Dogs

Many dogs have become famous through acts of heroism or great loyalty. Greyfriars Bobby is famous for following his master's coffin and sitting faithfully by the grave from 1858 until his own death some years later. There is a statue of him in a churchyard in Edinburgh, Scotland.

Barry was a famous St Bernard who rescued at least 40 travelers lost in the snow-covered mountain passes of the Alps.

A famous dog of modern times is Laika, the dog that orbited the Earth in a Russian spaceship. Rin Tin Tin was the first dog film star, and later Lassie became just as famous. Cartoon dogs like Pluto and Snoopy have also become very well known.

▶ **Family tree** This family tree shows how the dog is descended from the wolf. Another close relative is the fox. The jackal and hyena are also part of the family.

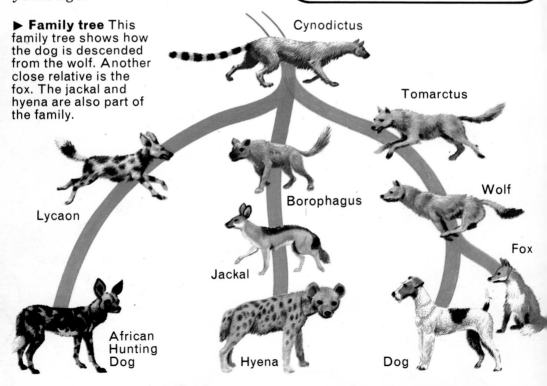

Cynodictus

Tomarctus

Wolf

Fox

Lycaon

Borophagus

Jackal

African Hunting Dog

Hyena

Dog

Wild Dogs

Different types of wild dog live in different parts of the world. Wolves are found in USA, Asia, Canada and a few places in Europe. They used to live in Britain too, but the last ones were killed over 200 years ago. Wolves hunt in packs and help each other to kill animals much larger than themselves.

Jackals also live in packs. But they are mainly scavengers, eating the remains of larger animals. They roam in parts of Asia, Europe and Africa. The coyote hunts on the plains of North America and the dingo hunts in Australia.

▼ **Dingo** This wild dog lives in Australia.

▶ **Jackal** It lives in Asia, Africa and southeastern Europe.

▶ **Coyote** It lives on the Prairies of North America where it hunts small mammals.

▼ **Timber Wolf** This wolf from North America is also called the Gray Wolf. Like all wolves it hunts in packs.

Sporting Dogs

Pointers, setters, retrievers and spaniels are all gundogs. They were bred for finding or retrieving game. Pointers go ahead of the sportsman to find the game. When they scent birds, they freeze like a statue, pointing towards the hidden game. Setters do the same. But, like many other gundogs, they are not used very much for this work now. Retrievers find and fetch dead game. They are expected to carry it back to the sportsman without damaging it. Spaniels work through thick cover, flushing out game.

Setters

English Setter

Irish Setter

Gordon Setter

▼ **Chesapeake Bay Retriever**
It is an excellent swimmer.

▼ **Black Labrador**
Labradors have a glossy coat and can also be yellow.

▲ **Golden Retriever**
This gentle dog makes a good family pet.

Spaniels

▲ Springer Spaniel
An active gun dog, the Springer also makes a good pet.

▲ Cocker Spaniel
A very popular family pet.

▲ Brittany Spaniel
An intelligent gundog from France.

▲ American Water Spaniel An excellent water dog.

▲ Field Spaniel
It is one of the lesser-known spaniels.

▲ Irish Water Spaniel
This dog is the tallest of the spaniels.

▼ Weimaraner The silver-gray Weimaraner came from Germany.

▼ German Short-haired Pointer
This pointer also retrieves dead game.

▼ Pointer
Pointers are built to gallop over the ground.

Hounds

Hounds can be divided into two types: the sight hounds and the scent hounds. The sight hounds are built for speed with long, slender bodies. They have to be able to outrun their prey. Sight hounds include some of the oldest breeds, like the Saluki which is mentioned as early as 3000 BC.

Scent hounds are more heavily built. They find their prey by following its scent until they wear it out. They do not have to run fast but they must have great stamina when tracking down animals. Scent hounds usually hunt in packs. They were used in the past for hunting many animals, including deer, wild boar and otters. Today some scent hounds are still used for hunting foxes and hares.

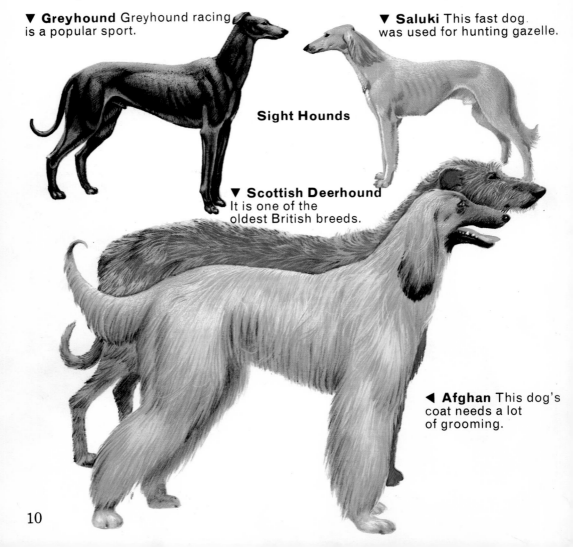

▼ **Greyhound** Greyhound racing is a popular sport.

▼ **Saluki** This fast dog was used for hunting gazelle.

Sight Hounds

▼ **Scottish Deerhound** It is one of the oldest British breeds.

◄ **Afghan** This dog's coat needs a lot of grooming.

Scent Hounds

Smooth-haired

Long-haired

▼ **Basset Hound** It came from France and once hunted hares.

◄ **Dachshunds** were used for hunting badgers.

▼ **Otterhound** A rare breed of dog.

◄ **Coonhound** It is used for raccoon hunting.

◄ **Beagle** It is now a popular pet.

▼ **Bloodhounds** have remarkable scenting powers.

▲ **Harrier** It was once bred to hunt hares.

11

Terriers

Almost all the breeds of terrier are British. Many of the breeds are named after places. This is because when a good terrier was bred many people wanted one of the pups. So all the terriers in one area were often related.

Terriers were once used to hunt vermin like rats and polecats. They were expected to dig the vermin out of their holes. Some terriers were carried on horseback while the hounds followed the scent of a fox. The terriers were then sent down the fox's hole to chase it out from its refuge.

▲ **Scottish Terrier** Usually these dogs are black but they can be *wheaten* or *brindle*.

▲ **Australian Terrier** A small but courageous dog.

▼ **Fox Terrier** A gay and lively dog.

▼ **Welsh Terrier** Like all terriers it is strong and hardy.

◄ **Irish Terrier** Nicknamed the "Red Devil" because of its fighting spirit.

▼ **Kerry Blue Terrier** An affectionate terrier from Ireland.

▼ **Manchester Terrier** It is one of the few smooth-coated terriers.

Sealyham This white-coated terrier came from Wales.

▲ **Cairn Terrier** This breed killed vermin in Scotland.

▲ **Norwich Terrier** A lively and friendly dog.

▲ **Dandie Dinmont** It comes from the Border country of Scotland.

▲ **Skye Terrier** It is a good watchdog.

▲ **West Highland White** An all-white Scottish breed.

Bedlington The lamb-like appearance of the Bedlington hides its sporting nature.

▼ **Bull Terrier** This terrier was once used for dog fighting.

▼ **Border Terrier** This dog needs little in the way of grooming.

▶ **Airedale** The largest of the terrier group.

Working Dogs

▲ **Huskies** used to be the only means of transport in the Arctic.

Working dogs include all of the sheepdogs, guard dogs and "draft" dogs (ones used for pulling sleds and carts). Many of these breeds are also used for police and army work and for guiding the blind.

The sheepdogs vary greatly in appearance as they live and work under different conditions. The Australian sheepdog, the Kelpie, is a light muscular animal which often has to run over the backs of tightly packed sheep. Other sheepdogs, like the Briard and the Puli, have very heavy coats to protect them against very cold weather.

Guard dogs, like the Rottweiler and the German Shepherd Dog, were once sheep and cattle dogs. They have only recently been used as police and army dogs.

▼ **St Bernard** This dog once used to guide travelers across snowbound passes in the Alps.

▼ **Bernese Mountain Dog** It used to pull carts of produce to market in Switzerland.

▼ **Newfoundland** A good-natured, gentle dog and a powerful swimmer.

▶ **Samoyed** It used to herd reindeer and pull sleds in Siberia.

▶ **Great Dane** This huge dog came from Germany.

▶ **Boxer** A guard dog.

Collie It is now bred for show rather than work.

▲ **Doberman** A good guard dog.

▲ **German Shepherd Dog** The most popular breed in the world.

▼ **Rottweiler** This dog is used for police and army work.

▼ **Briard** A French sheepdog.

▲ **Bouvier des Flandres** A large French sheepdog.

◀ **Kelpie** An Australian sheepdog.

▼ **Belgian Sheepdog** A hardworking sheepdog.

Pembroke

▼ **Puli** It was used as a sheepdog in Hungary.

Cardigan

▲ **Corgis,** used as cattle dogs in Wales, make good pets.

▶ **Old English Sheepdog** Nicknamed the "Bobtail"

▲ **Pekingese** These dogs make tough and playful pets.

▲ **Affenpinscher** Dogs of this old German breed make good companions.

▲ **Yorkshire Terrier** Its silky coat needs a lot of care.

▲ **Maltese Ter** One of the olde European toy b

Toy Dogs

Toy dogs are so called because they are all very small. Tiny dogs have always been popular. Throughout the centuries they have been bred for companionship and amusement.

The Ancient Egyptians buried toy dogs in the graves of their royalty. English Kings and Queens have almost always owned toy dogs. The King Charles Spaniel is named after King Charles II. In China, many years ago, only royal families could own a Pekingese. Some were small enough to be carried in their owners' sleeves. In earlier times, lap dogs helped to

▼ **Brussels Griffon** This Belgian dog makes a lively pet.

▼ **Italian Greyhound** This graceful dog was a court favourite in many of the capitals of Europe.

▼ **Chihuahua** This breed came from Mexico and can be either long- or smooth-coated.

▼ **Australian Silky Terrier** It is also known as the Sydney Silky.

▲ **English Toy Spaniel**
In Britain this dog is known as the King Charles Spaniel.

▲ **Cavalier King Charles Spaniel** It is one of the largest toy breeds.

▲ **Japanese Spaniel** This short-faced dog can be either black and white or red and white.

▲ **Pomeranian** Its foxy face is framed by a ruff of hair.

keep their owners warm. It was also widely believed that the dogs would attract their mistress's fleas.

Most toy breeds have long histories. Many of the short-nosed breeds, like the Pekingese, the Japanese Spaniel and the Pug, came from the Far East many years ago. The Maltese Terrier's history goes back to the pre-Christian era.

Some toy dogs like the Italian Greyhound and the Miniature Pinscher are small versions of larger breeds. Others like the Pomeranian were once much larger dogs. Their smaller puppies were specially chosen and bred. The larger dogs eventually died out.

▼ **Toy Poodles** can have a wide variety of colors but they must always be less than 10 in tall at the shoulder.

▶ **Miniature Pinscher**
Dogs of this German breed make good watchdogs.

▶ **Papillon** Its large ears give this dog its name, which is French for butterfly.

17

Dogs for Pets

The dogs shown on this page are some of those from a group known as utility dogs. These are breeds which do not easily fit into any of the other groups. Utility dogs all make good pets. Most of the dogs pictured throughout the book will also make good pets, as long as you choose wisely.

One of the main reasons for keeping a dog as a pet is for the friendship it provides. Dogs like company so it is not really right to keep one at all if it will have to be shut up alone for long periods every day. Some dogs, especially those built for speed, need a lot of exercise every day and large dogs cost a lot of money to feed. The very tiny breeds need care as they are more easily hurt when you are playing with them. Long-haired breeds bring in a lot of mud. This may not be popular with whoever does the housework. These breeds also need more care taken of their coats. These are all the things you should think about when choosing a dog.

◀ **Dalmatian** This good natured dog used to trot between the wheels of horse-drawn carriage

▼ **Boston Terrier** Dogs of this breed make good house pets and companions.

▲ **Chow Chow** One of the special features of this Chinese dog is its black tongue.

◀ **French Bulldog** It does not need much grooming or exercise.

18

▼ **Poodles** come in three different sizes: Standard, Miniature and Toy (see page 17). These fun-loving dogs have to be clipped from time to time and brushed daily.

Puppy-clipped Poodle

Lion-clipped Poodle

▶ **Schipperke** Once used on canal barges in Belgium, this dog now makes a good family pet.

▼ **Bulldog** Its fierce face disguises a friendly nature.

▼ **Lhasa Apso** This dog was once used as a watchdog in Tibet.

▲ **Keeshond** Once a barge dog in Holland, the Keeshond is now popular as a pet.

Looking After a Dog

A new puppy is not a toy that you can order about and play with all the time. Puppies need a lot of sleep and they should have their own bed where they will not be disturbed.

Most dogs love human company and enjoy playing. Your pet should be exercised every day. Never allow your dog to run loose on the roads. This is dangerous to the dog and to drivers.

▲ **Bedding** Your dog should have its own bed in a quiet, draft free corner where it can sleep in peace when it wants. The pug in the picture rests in a cane basket. The bedding should be washed once a week. You should not allow your dog to sleep in your bed.

▼ **Grooming** keeps a dog healthy as well as smart. You should have no problems with a long-haired dog, like the Shih Tzu pictured, if it is groomed daily. You will need a special brush and comb. Short-haired dogs need only a brush or a hound glove. Nail clippers are sometimes necessary but you will need to be shown how to use them by an expert.

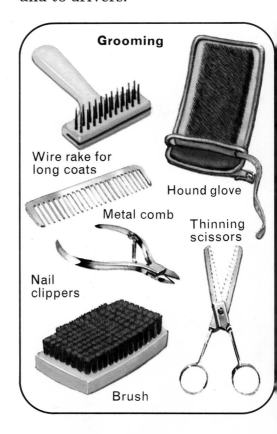

Grooming

Wire rake for long coats

Hound glove

Metal comb

Thinning scissors

Nail clippers

Brush

Long-haired breeds need grooming daily whereas short-haired ones can be done once a week. Puppies need frequent feeding but adult dogs need only one meal a day, preferably in the evening. All dogs need a bowl of fresh water that they can get to at all times.

Many dogs enjoy car rides but they should never be left shut in a car that is standing in the sun. In a short time it can get very hot inside the car. Some dogs have died in such cases. If your dog is well trained you can take it almost anywhere and you will have a pet to be proud of.

Feeding and Drinking
Your dog should have its own bowl and never eat out of the family's dishes. You should not feed it between meals or give it tidbits from the table. Big raw bones or hard biscuits will help clean your dog's teeth. Always make sure that your dog has a bowl of water. Puppies, like the ones below, can be given milk as part of their diet.

Rolled leather collar

Choke chain

Trigger clip

Decorative collar

▲ **Collars and Leashes** Your dog should always wear a collar with its name and your address on it. You should keep the dog on the leash whenever there are cars around. The best and strongest leash clip is the trigger clip shown above.

Training a Dog

Dogs enjoy the right kind of training. While they are being taught or performing they are getting attention from you, which all dogs love. A dog that will come when it is called, walk quietly by your side, and sit and lie down when it is told is much more fun to own. A dog that you have trained yourself will also feel closer to you than one which is allowed to do whatever it wants.

Lessons should be kept short and held often. You will need to be patient and show your dog what to do. Only try to teach one thing at a time. Try also to end each lesson with something your dog does well so that you can give it a lot of praise.

The first thing your dog should learn is its name. Call your puppy often and reward it with praise, a tidbit or a game. Always make it pleasant for the dog to come to you. If you want to scold the animal go up to it so that it does not think it is being scolded for coming to you. Puppies have to become used to a collar and leash but encouragement will soon teach it to enjoy walking with you.

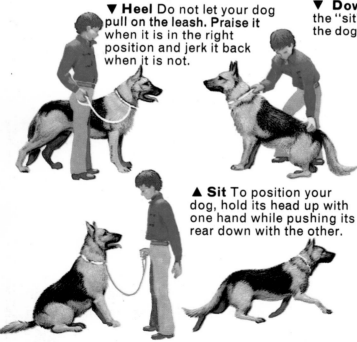

▼ **Heel** Do not let your dog pull on the leash. Praise it when it is in the right position and jerk it back when it is not.

▲ **Sit** To position your dog, hold its head up with one hand while pushing its rear down with the other.

▼ **Down** This should be taught once the "sit" has been learned. Gently slide the dog's forepaws out from under it.

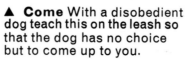

▲ **Stay** Stand in front of your dog to stop it moving until you tell it that it may. Gradually increase the distance.

▲ **Come** With a disobedient dog teach this on the leash so that the dog has no choice but to come up to you.

▲ **Do's and Don'ts** Do praise your dog for every success however small. Don't ever get irritable or lose your temper.

Glossary

Brindle Brown with streaks of a darker color or black.

Carnivore A meat-eating animal. Dogs are carnivores.

Choke chain A slip collar used for training. It needs to be put on correctly and used correctly to be useful.

Cropping Cutting the outside flap off a dog's ear to produce a small upright ear. Cropping is illegal in some countries.

Dew claws The fifth claw found a little way up the leg in some breeds of dog.

Docking Cutting off the tail of the dog to reduce its natural length.

Droving Herding cattle over long distances before the days of road and rail transport.

Feathering The fringes of hair on the backs of the legs and under the tail.

Gait The way a dog moves.

Mask Dark shading on the nose of some breeds.

Merle A gray mixture flecked or streaked with black.

Mongrel An animal whose ancestors are not purebred.

Pedigree An animal whose ancestry is known and recorded and which when mated to one of its own breed will reproduce its own type.

Purebred See under *pedigree*.

Ruff The stiff frill of hair round a dog's neck as in the Chow.

Sable Black-tipped hairs over a golden or fawn base color.

Wheaten Fawn.

Withers The point where the neck joins the back. The height of both dogs and horses is measured from this point to the ground.

Index